WITCHES IN THE WORKPLACE

HOW TO BUILD AN EFFECTIVE BATTLE STRATEGY

AND WIN

ALTAR BOOKS
A DIVISION OF

QUIVERFULL
PUBLISHING

Yvonne D. Camper

Cover Photo: Toa Heftiba, Unsplash

WITCHES IN THE WORKPLACE

HOW TO BUILD AN EFFECTIVE BATTLE STRATEGY AND WIN

Yvonne D. Camper

Chapter 1

MIRACLE IN THE MARKETPLACE

Moses was promoted because God heard the cry of the people. Exodus 3:7 (NIV) says, "*The LORD said, "I have indeed seen the misery of my people in Egypt. I have heard them crying out because of their slave drivers, and I am concerned about their suffering.*"

He saw how Pharoah was mistreating them and using them to push his agenda and build his kingdom. God was incensed by Pharoah's behavior and was ready to respond to the injustice. As only God can do. He orchestrated a divine departure out of Egypt and the miracle of the Red Sea.

Expect a miracle in the marketplace because God has heard your cry. I believe the greatest revival is not going to be confined in the four walls of a church but out in the marketplace where Jesus spent the majority of His time. Ridley College wrote an article called, "Why did Jesus spend so much time in the marketplace? The article says,

Typically, we might think of our faith as being personal, spiritual, and private; however, as we read the Gospel accounts, we see that Jesus saw relationship with God as something worked out in community, that affected every area of life, and was lived out in public.

In 1857 businessman, Joseph Lanphier spearheaded a noon-time prayer which sparked an American revival. The Fulton Church's noontime prayer and outpouring led to a reported 1 million souls being saved from coast to coast and continent to continent. So many prophets are being targeted for deletion in the marketplace. They have been overlooked for promotions, denied advancement, and fired because the enemy is afraid of their prophetic power and influence. The enemy's goal is to keep you oppressed and suppressed just like Pharoah did to the Israelites. He wants to silence your voice and to stop the coming marketplace revival.

I see new businesses, new jobs, and divine connections being established. Jesus said, "Don't you have a saying, 'It's still four months until harvest'? I tell you, open your eyes and look at the fields! They are ripe for harvest (NIV).

I decree today, by the authority of the Holy Ghost, that liberation is coming to everyone that hears the clarion call. I decree the plans of every witch and warlock that is trying to shut you down be frustrated. I declare raises, promotions, favor, new jobs, advancements, and the release of resources.

God is removing every person who has been standing in your way and opposing you. Spells, hexes, and curses are being broken today. The environment around us is rapidly shifting, depression, fear, anxiety, and confusion are being lifted right now. It is time to advance!

notes

_____

_____

_____

_____

_____

_____

_____

_____

_____

_____

_____

_____

_____

Chapter 2

THE MARKETPLACE PROPHET

As a marketplace prophet, it took me many years to find my niche. Most of the jobs I had were short-lived, and I was incredibly bored until I landed my first job in a reputable Healthcare organization doing Project Management, Organizational Development, and Process Improvement. The work was so intriguing to me because it offered me the opportunity to bring order to chaos, allowing me to take abstract data and make it into something meaningful.

According to Deuteronomy 34:10, Moses was the most significant prophet until Jesus, but he spent much of his time leading, teaching, settling disputes, and organizing the people so that God's plan could be executed. As a marketplace prophet, you must understand Matthew 13:38, this passage reminds us the field is the world, not the church. This implies you will spend the bulk of your time in the workforce. Understanding Moses' responsibilities tell you one of a prophet's greatest strengths is their ability to establish order and structure to their environment.

This hard wiring can sometimes be misconstrued as being bossy, nitpicky, or controlling, which is a threat to people who struggle with inadequacy. It will also uncover and expose people who are not doing their jobs. Many times, in the Bible, God-sanctioned a prophet to speak because things were out of order and not in sync with His divine plan.

The Ten Commandments are a systematic document that brought order to worship because the people's worship was disorderly. God was always reminding the children of Israel that He was the only God that was supposed to be worshipped.

So, for the past thirty years, I have found myself bringing order to the marketplace, which has not been without a fight. I had to continually remind myself and meditate on

Psalms 35:1 (NASB), "*... Contend, O LORD, with those who contend with me; Fight against those who fight against me.*"

So, prophet, do not be alarmed if everywhere you go is chaotic; it is God's plan, and you are on a divine assignment. Prophets do not come onto the scene until it is time to build up or tear down a work. God admonished Jeremiah,

> *Behold, I have put My words in your mouth. See, I have appointed you today over nations and kingdoms to uproot and tear down, to destroy and overthrow, to build and plant* (Berean Study Bible).

Every single place where God sent me was either newly established, changing their infrastructure, or in the middle of a building program. Over the years I realized how I was divinely and strategically placed in every organization.

In a healthy organization, you can very quickly become an integral part of the core leadership which can often create strained relationships and expose jealousy and envy. This innate gifting will upset and intimidate those that want to, for the wrong reasons, be close to the boss.

Therefore, be mindful of the employees that appear to be initially overly friendly and helpful because envy masquerades itself as interest. Unfortunately, today most organizations are not healthy because an organization is only as healthy as the people in it. Your marketplace assignment is to come alongside leadership and help keep the people engaged during times of upheaval and change. Due to your sensitivity to the Spirit and keen discernment, you can ward off sneak attacks from the enemy that would hamper growth and potentially cause discord among the people.

You will also add vibrancy, strength, and vigor to the people by refreshing them with your spiritual discipline and power-packed words. That is why many times, in the marketplace, Prophets will be the first to volunteer for a new project and organize department functions to rally and motivate the people which can be misconstrued by your peers that you are trying to upstage them.

As a marketplace Prophet on a previous assignment, I found myself struggling with my new boss, and I could not figure out why. I had a dream in which she told me to be back from lunch in 30-minutes. I was desperately trying to get back on time, but I lost my keys, my purse and ended up in a completely unfamiliar building. In the dream my anxiety level was debilitating.

When I awoke, I had to step away from the situation to see what the real problem was. I finally understood if my assignment was to bring order, then the enemy's counterattack was to create confusion. The Holy Spirit revealed to me who the real person was behind these assaults because I thought it was someone else, as well as uncover the enemy's strategy. This information empowered me to reposition myself.

Whenever God wanted to stop progress, He sent confusion. Deuteronomy 28:20 says, *"The LORD will send on you cursing, confusion, and rebuke in all that you set your hand to do."* The enemy has always mirrored and copied

God's battle strategy. In a state of confusion, you cannot think clearly; you are disoriented, and you have trouble focusing and making decisions. Chaos is the enemy's attack, but your counterattack is establishing divine order. [1]

---

[1] Yvonne D. Camper. Healing the Wounds Prophetic Leadership Transformed. Quiver Full Publishing, 2017

_____
_____
_____
_____
_____
_____
_____
_____
_____
_____
_____
_____
_____

Chapter 3

WHAT IS A WITCH?

There are real, active, and functioning witches in the workplace who are on assignment just like you are. But for this book, I am referring to people who use emotional manipulation to maintain their power. They use fear, intimidation, control, and bullying to get what they want. They often struggle with jealousy, envy, and a broken self-image.

They are always trying to feed their shattered egos, and absolutely no one else can be the center of attention. I do also agree that there are people that have actually turned their souls over to the enemy for power. These practicing witches will be discussed in a later chapter.

I also want to address the topic of a Christian Witch. These are people who pretend to be believers. They know all of the church lingo and behavior but have not been truly converted on the inside by the Holy Spirit. Jesus rebuked the Sadducees and Pharisees saying in Matthew 23:27 (NIV),

Woe to you, teachers of the law and Pharisees, you hypocrites! You are like whitewashed tombs, which look beautiful on the outside but on the inside are full of the bones of the dead and everything unclean.

They can be very deceptive and hard to detect because they look like and smell like Christians but do not demonstrate the nature of Christ. They are extremely helpful and seem to be jubilant in their relationship with Christ, but it is a demonic front. They are probably more dangerous than a person that does not know Christ. The reason being is because they have the unique opportunity to get close to you fairly quickly. By the time you recognize them it is too late, and you have already been bitten.

For those that have not accepted Christ sabotage is their weapon of choice. They can be very genuine and kind people until they feel threatened or sense they are losing influence. Many of them genuinely think they are friendly people, and they are, to those they feel superior to or those that are willing to play the game. These individuals are lost, deadly, and are in desperate need of a savior. They are prime candidates for the Gospel of Jesus Christ and are our present mission field. I will discuss in detail the subject of the Christian Witch phenomena in the next chapter.

Because the workplace has become one of Satan's biggest battlegrounds, we must be able to identify the enemy. As believers, we are supposed to love and disciple the people in our workplace, but we also have to use wisdom, so we do not fall into the enemy's trap.

_____
_____
_____
_____
_____
_____
_____
_____
_____
_____
_____
_____
_____

Chapter 4

THE ANATOMY OF A CHRISTIAN WITCH

There has been an insurgence of so-called Christian Witches in the last decade or so. This would also include false prophets. I would attribute it to two things. First Church wounds and secondly Satan's attack against the church and the people of God. We must understand that Witchcraft is evil and there is no such thing as a good witch. Daniel 7:25 says,

He shall speak pompous words against the Most High, Shall persecute the saints of the Most High, And shall intend to change times and law. Then the saints shall be given into his hand For a time and times and half a time(NKJV).

Abusive leadership in the church is at an all-time high and people are fed up. I believe some of these people genuinely love the Lord but because they have been bound and indoctrinated by Pimps over the pulpit who control the masses with religion, there is an element of guilt in standing up and exercising your God-given right to be respected and free in the liberty Christ died for.

So, instead of responding to these assaults healthily, these individuals lean towards manipulation and control to get their way or ease their pain. Webster defines a witch as, "*A witch, is one that is credited with malignant powers especially a woman practicing black magic with the aid of the devil or a familiar spirit.*"

The deception is they are not doing evil or partnering with satanic forces. These people are deceived into believing they are not practicing sorcery and what they are doing is right. Witchcraft is not a Spirit but is a work of the flesh according to the Apostle Paul (Galatians 5:16-21). People can partner with demonic spirits if they are not careful but much of it is willful as a means to gain power that has been lost or taken.

Witchcraft is usually the result of an emotional or sexual trauma caused by someone in authority. To counteract the assault, they need to access a power higher than theirs to get revenge on their perpetrators. But what generally happens is they are afraid to confront their assailants and use this power on everyone they feel threatened by. It becomes a way of life for them. They can oftentimes be very transient, going from place to place until they get found out. Once they have been uncovered, they search out their next victim.

The reason it is so difficult for these people to get free is that they have exchanged their pain for pride. There is a spirit of deception that is confusing the people of God into thinking they can practice witchcraft and Christianity at the same time. So, what is a Biblical Christian? It is one who follows the teachings of Jesus. They believe in the validity of the Bible and embrace the ministry of the Holy Spirit. With their confession of Jesus as Lord, there is an outward manifestation of what they believe. You cannot be a Christian and get your palms read, call psychic hotlines, read your horoscope, use crystals, or sage to cleanse the atmosphere. These activities open demonic doors in a person's life.

A Christian seeks God for information. Witches look for forms of weaknesses in a person or organization where they can gain control. They seek to cause division and strife. As Christians, we come to bring peace and unity. Witchcrafts ultimate desire is to bring destruction. They weaponize peoples hurts and use it as a means of control. The spirit of witchcraft in the Bible is linked to Queen Jezebel. She was a false prophetess or spirit that sought to control and destroy people in power, especially spiritual power so that she could execute her plan.

According to the Bible, there are legal forms of accessing the spiritual realm and illegal forms of accessing the spiritual realm. We must understand as Christians the plumbline is the word of God. America is being repackaged and what used to be a Christian nation is now becoming more post-modernistic, meaning if I think it is true then it is true. Many are rejecting Christianity, so people are desperately looking for something to fill the God void. Witchcraft is attractive, especially to millennials.

It is being represented as something innocent and empowering. It is no longer presented as evil and demonic. This new breed promotes free thought and the love of nature. It is giving them the false sense that they can worship God any way they want to. As a Christian you must read the word of God regularly, Timothy said, "*All Scripture is God-breathed and is useful for teaching, rebuking, correcting and training in righteousness,*" (Timothy 3:16, NIV).

In the workplace many of you are believing God for a promotion, therefore, the enemy is going to do everything he can to thwart the plan of God in your life. The marketplace is being flooded with this illegal activity and these predatory people. But God promised that He would give you the land. He also admonished you not to be conformed to the spirit of this age. You cannot fight an insult with an insult or a slight for a slight, but you overcome evil with good.

_____

_____

_____

_____

_____

_____

_____

_____

_____

_____

_____

_____

Chapter 5

WHAT IS WITCHCRAFT?

It is essential to understand the history of witchcraft and know what it is. Knowing what you are dealing with will help you fortify yourself and build an effective battle strategy. Witchcraft according to I Samuel 15:23 is a sin and complete rebellion against God. Witchcraft is a form of spiritual warfare against a believer, and the *craft* is the primary use of incantations, spells, curses, the use of food and objects to snare their prey.

The Bible also refers to it as magic, soothsaying, or fortune-telling. These practices are forbidden by God and in a previous society were considered illegal. Seeking supernatural powers outside of God has been practiced throughout the ages and is a form of divination. It is accessing the spiritual realm illegally. Leviticus 19:31 (NIV) warns us, "'*Do not turn to mediums or seek out spiritists, for you will be defiled by them. I am the LORD your God.*'"

So, how does *witchcraft* work, and what is it? It is a stolen Biblical principle; it is utilizing the power of words. Incantations are merely words concocted to influence a person against their will. Chants are words spoken or unspoken that are believed to invoke a hex, spell, or mojo. Curses are words intended to evoke a supernatural power to inflict harm or punishment. The words we speak are powerful. Proverbs 18:21 (MSG) says, "*Words kill, words give life; they're either poison or fruit—you choose."* Satan has always used and perverted Biblical principles to advance his agenda.

These Witches in the Workplace, many times, do not possess any innate spiritual abilities, nor do they have power or authority. They, knowingly or unknowing, solicit the help of demonic spirits to do their bidding. What people often feel is the presence of the spirit of fear which manifests itself in intimidation and anxiety. These deadly assaults can produce physical and emotional symptoms like heart palpitations, insomnia, depression, confusion, and fatigue.

It is important to understand that the main objective of workplace warfare is their advancement and your removal. These people want to shine and be the best and the brightest. They want the full attention of the people in charge and will use any tactic available to crush their opponent. In their eyes, you are standing in the way and they need you gone so they can have complete control and authority. Jezebel needed Elijah out of the way because he was the only one who could rival her power. It is also imperative to understand if God placed you, no one can replace you. If

The scope of this book is to help you survive and flourish in the marketplace and help you identify and dismantle the work of the enemy. This is hand-to-hand combat and spiritual warfare, which I will discuss in a later chapter, can be exhausting if you do not have an effective strategy. Exodus 22:18 (KJV) says, "*Thou shalt not suffer a witch to live.*"

notes

_____

_____

_____

_____

_____

_____

_____

_____

_____

_____

_____

_____

Chapter 6

WITCHES, WARLOCKS AND PSYCHICS IN THE WORKPLACE, WHY AM I A TARGET?

The workplace in the last 30 years or so has become increasingly more volatile. I believe part of it is that many believers did not understand that their spiritual assignment could be in the marketplace and not just in the church. Work was just an opportunity to fulfill their financial obligations. I remember praying to God begging Him to remove me from the marketplace.

I read a quote that said, "*Think of your career as your ministry. Make your work an expression of love and service to mankind.*" That was a foreign concept to me. If we consider only 2% of people work in the church, then where are the other 98%? They are in the marketplace, whether they work for a company or own their own company.

The more you are called to this workplace ministry the more spiritual warfare escalates. The reason you have become a target is that these evil spirits are heavily influencing people who are afraid you are going to disrupt their atmosphere with your presence. What they recognize is your anointing and spiritual authority. In my tenure in the marketplace, while working for another company, the Holy Spirit in me began to expose the diabolical plans and assignments of my boss. It was not intentional. I was just doing the job they hired me for.

Another reason is that you can be too trusting so you can fit in. God does not want you to fit in, He wants you to stand out. The workplace is filled with low-trust people. Co-workers are not your friends they do not have the right to access any personal information from you and you cannot create unhealthy connections with these people. Never go to a job and be an open book. The more information they have about you the more they can develop a strategic plan against you. When you go into new environments you share only what the Holy Spirit tells you to for the purpose of evangelism.

In my experience, the first person to buddy up to you is the person you should watch out for. They are sizing you up and examining their competition. They will be the first to turn on you. This is where dialoguing with the Holy Spirit becomes crucial. I also want to encourage you about what you post on Social Media. Privacy is an asset not a liability. I decided I would choose the people that would be in my life and no longer let people choose me. I also, learned that I had every right in Christ to protect and cover myself, that is not pride it is wisdom.

As Christians sometimes we believe we have to be doormats to spread the Gospel but that was not Jesus' modus operandi, Jesus had clear boundaries and was not afraid to make them known. Be observant and evaluate the culture before you get involved, see how people interact with each other. Look how managers talk to their subordinates. Broken and wounded people can become extremely vicious.

If you have settled the fact that you are on a divine assignment, ask God why he sent you to this job? What are you supposed to accomplish, who are you supposed to meet? What is your responsibility spiritually, professionally, and socially? Many times, God will send you to places never for the reasons you think. My last professional assignment launched me into what I am doing now. My VP said, "*Your current job is training you for your next job.*" If your time is up, ask God what your next move is? One woman wrote on my Youtube and said, "*When I quit my job, I am taking my good energy with me.*" Jesus admonished his disciples if they do not receive you shake the dust and take your peace with you (Matthew 10:13-14).

The Bible says we will be sheep among wolves. So, be encouraged when you are sent to environments that are toxic and volatile. In 1 Corinthians 16:19, Paul talks about how he was presented with a great opportunity, but there were devils at the open door. Joshua had to go into the promised land and drive out all the enemies. Many times, warfare and conflict are an indication that you are in your assignment. So, dig in your heals and accomplish your assignment.

_____
_____
_____
_____
_____
_____
_____
_____
_____
_____
_____
_____

CHAPTER 7

HOW TO IDENTIFY A WITCH IN THE WORKPLACE

Workplace bullying has become the norm in our society. The problem with it is most companies will not mitigate these issues or support the employees that are being bullied. I believe one of the main culprits is insecurity and intimidation by those in leadership.

Witches can often be unregenerate prophetic people who use their gifts for evil. Romans 11:29 (MSG) says, "*God's gifts and God's call are under full warranty – never canceled, never rescinded.*" This scripture means, we can do whatever we choose with the gifts and talents God gives us. We can either use them for good or for evil. We can use them to bless people or use them to hurt people.

Most of these witches in the workplace struggle with narcissism, which is a term we hear a lot about today. Psychology Today's definition of narcissism is, "*Narcissism is characterized by a grandiose sense of self-importance, a lack of empathy for others, a need for excessive admiration, and the belief that one is unique and deserving of special treatment.*

Identifying these individuals is half the battle. Their responsibility is to stay hidden because operating in darkness is their greatest ally. Also, learning to trust our discernment is extremely important. When we ignore our gut, many times it is a religious spirit perverting the word of God. The go-to scripture most people use to manipulate God's people is Mark 12:30-31 (NIV), which says,

Love the Lord your God with all your heart and with all your soul and with all your mind and with all your strength.' The second is this: 'Love your neighbor as yourself.' There is no commandment greater than these.

I learned that we have to love ourselves first! Love is not synonymous with abuse. I can love a person and protect myself at the same time. The characteristics below can help you identify those that operate in a spirit of witchcraft:

o They are very manipulative both verbally and emotionally.

o In the face of conflict, it is difficult to speak with them because they railroad all conversations. Their objective is to create confusion and redirect blame.

o They always strive to be right, and it is hard for them to accept responsibility for their own mistakes.

o Nothing they say is valid, and when confronted they never know what you are talking about and pretend to be innocent.

o They are almost always gossipers and liars.

o They struggle with deep-seated anger issues and seem to have a very damaged self-image.

o They can be genuinely nice and kind but defensive when they feel threatened or controlled.

o Many of them have very unhealthy family relationships.

o They are often overly critical of and demean their subordinates.

o They seek to invalidate people and shake their confidence.

o They often show signs of jealousy and envy with other co-workers or subordinates.

o Most of their communication is verbal. These individuals often avoid written emails. If they do use email, you can never resolve anything with them, and the barrage of meaningless emails never ends.

o They are sticklers for detail, they readily recognize others' mistakes and hide their own.

o Initially, they are very friendly as they size you up, looking for any weakness on which they can capitalize.

o They initially appear to be extremely helpful.

o Selfish ambition drives everything they do.

_____
_____
_____
_____
_____
_____
_____
_____
_____
_____
_____
_____

CHAPTER 8

ANATOMY OF AN ASSAULT

According, to a study conducted at Kaiser Permanente, which is one of the largest healthcare organizations in the country, 88% of all people had either seen workplace bullying or have been a victim of it. Sadly, workplace bullying has become the norm today. So often, prophets can be the target of these vicious assaults.

I base my previous statement on my own experience as well as speaking with other marketplace prophets. They tend to wear the bull's eye because they are not comfortable with the status quo and tend to challenge the system. Another reason they can be the target is that the enemy can detect that the Holy Spirit inside of them opposes their satanic agenda.

Towards the end of my marketplace career, I focused my energy on process improvement. Although that is what I was hired to do I quickly became an enemy of the state. My expertise began to expose her inadequacies, this created a lot of conflicts. It got to the point where it was difficult for her to speak to me directly unless it was necessary. I became her biggest threat. Her hiring strategy was to hire people that would cover and protect her. Unfortunately for her, God hired me, and I refused to get involved in office politics. I preferred to do the work I was hired to for.

Instead, my suggestions for improvement only served to create endless angst, and the powers that be wanted me gone. At that point, I had to discern if this was a time for me to contend for my position or was God moving me on? I had fought many battles within that organization, and God prevailed every single time. This particular battle was different, and I knew it was time for me to move on.

What Satan meant for evil, God used it for my good (Genesis 50:20). Satan's final assault within that organization launched me into divine purpose. The tactics utilized to remove me were far less than ethical and very hurtful. Their agenda was "by any means necessary," but I understood that what God had given me could not be taken away from me until He was finished.

Unfortunately, this particular attack took me off-guard, and I was not prepared for what would ensue over the coming months. Through that experience the Holy Spirit taught me the primary battle stance to take in dealing with a person who is operating in witchcraft is not to take the attack personally. Do not allow yourself to become a victim because victims are powerless.

With these individuals, the issue is more about their insecurities than it is about you. Either you intimidate them, or they fear you will outdo or expose them. They struggle with deep-seated identity issues. They are afraid of you and the one who lives inside of you. You must also recognize that you are encroaching on enemy territory.

You are not helpless in this situation and have every right to protect yourself and you do not have to accept their abuse. I understand that fear is a real component because we all have bills to pay and things to do. At this juncture in the fight, it is imperative you anchor yourself in the word. The word of God promises in Philippians 4:19 says, "*And my God will meet all your needs according to the riches of his glory in Christ Jesus* (NIV).

Recognizing the need for an effective battle strategy is vital. Spiritual warfare is part of every believer's daily agenda as much as attending a meeting, responding to emails, taking a conference call, or watching a webinar. If God placed you there, no one has the authority to displace you. Pray for your boss and look for another position if God so leads. Often, God will ask you to stay because He has a bigger plan. Or if it is time to go, He already has something prepared for you. Faith moves in darkness, many times we do not see what God is doing until we are courageous enough to take the first step. Your current job is setting the stage for your next assignment.

It is also important to remember you have the right to protect yourself. Do not allow the intimidation to keep you silent. Immediately report your boss' behavior to their boss, your company's compliance department, and or your Human Resources Department. I let the enemy torment me with silence far too long. My greatest business weapon was the ministry of documentation. Archive all email conversations. Use email as opposed to having phone conversations and document every single conversation as evidence.

People can refute and twist what you say but cannot defend themselves against things written on paper. You will find people who cooperate with this spirit want to always have clandestine meetings and secret gatherings so their behavior can go undetected.

notes

_____

_____

_____

_____

_____

_____

_____

_____

_____

_____

_____

_____

_____

_____

CHAPTER 9

UNDERSTANDING SPIRITUAL WARFARE

What is spiritual warfare? Spiritual warfare is uprooting the enemy from God's property and executing the Kingdom of God in your sphere of influence. In Luke 19:13 Jesus commanded his servants to do business and occupy until he returns. The earth and everything in it is bequeathed from Heaven and man is the designated guardian.

Jesus came to be our example of humility, authority, and dominion (1 Peter 2:21). For most of us, we will not, regularly, be physically attacked by demonic powers and spirits. 95% of warfare is psychological and the enemy is a master at. That is why it is important to renew your mind consistently to the fact the battle is already won.

Jesus' main assignment was to introduce the people to another way of living by walking in dominion and destroying the works of the devil (Colossians 2:15). He came to usher in a new world order, destroy the works of the enemy, dismantle archaic religious systems, shift governments, empower his people through the ministry of the Holy Spirit, and establish God's economy. Jesus always talked about The Kingdom of Heaven, The Kingdom of God and The Kingdom is Like. In Luke 4:33 (NIV), He said to them, "*I must preach the good news of the kingdom of God to the other towns as well; for I was sent for this purpose.*"

The Kingdom of God is His rule, realm, and authority. But as deputized believers, we have power over the rulers of darkness. He said in Luke 10:19 (LEB), "*Behold, I have given you the authority to tread on snakes and scorpions, and over all the power of the enemy, and nothing will ever harm you.*" Ephesians sets the framework for withstanding the work of the enemy.

The call to resist (6:10-13) – We are on the offensive, not the defensive.

The call to stand (6:14-17) – We have the weapons in our arsenal to stand firm.

The call to pray and be alert (18–20) – Pay attention and be discerning.

_____
_____
_____
_____
_____
_____
_____
_____
_____
_____
_____
_____
_____
_____

CHAPTER 10

NOT AGAINST FLESH AND BLOOD

The word of God reminds us that our fight is not against people but principalities, powers, and rulers of the demonic realm (Ephesians 6:20). Although it is easy to think it is a person, we must constantly remind ourselves that the battle is spiritual. Ask yourself the question, "Why am I under assault?" The short answer is the enemy is threatened by a spirit-filled believer because you are the only person that can rival its authority.

Since the battle is spiritual it must be fought from another plane. To be effective, it is important to understand the nature of the spiritual realm. One of the reasons demons do not have any authority is because, as previously mentioned, God put us in charge! The other reason is angels and demons are created beings and they are subject to the authority of God and men filled with God's spirits.

Psalms 148 talks about the Heavenly host in verse 5 it says, "*Let them praise the name of the LORD, for at his command they were created* (NIV). Therefore, in the creative order man is above angels and demons. We have complete dominion and authority to rule. We outrank Satan by position and authority (Psalms 8:5-6). Luke 10:17-18 (NIV) says,

The seventy-two returned with joy and said, "Lord, even the demons submit to us in Your name." So, He told them, "I saw Satan fall like lightning from heaven. Behold, I have given you authority to tread on snakes and scorpions, and over all the power of the enemy. Nothing will harm you.

When Satan fell a third of the angels went with him. Because of the fall, they lost their position and power and now desire to wreak havoc on the earth. Their greatest weapon of choice is people because they have the highest form of expression. Demons theologically are *fallen, angels.* They are hostile supernatural entities that seek to destroy and hinder the people of God. The good news is we have the victory! We are never without divine strength and angelic assistance.

When Elijah's servant got up one morning and saw the city surrounded by a great army, he was afraid and just knew they were doomed to destruction. But Elijah's response to God was Lord, "*Open his eyes.*" Let him see what I see, let him know that we are never alone. Elijah encouraged his servant and said in 2 Kings 6:15 (NIV), *"Do not be afraid,"* *Elisha answered, "for those who are with us are more than those who are with them."*

_____

_____

_____

_____

_____

_____

_____

_____

_____

_____

_____

_____

_____

CHAPTER 11

DEMONIC ACTIVITY IN THE MARKETPLACE

One of Satan's jobs is to torment the people of God, especially in the marketplace. Daniel says, "*He wants to wear the Saints out*" (Daniel 7;24). Why the marketplace? I believe the primary reason is the exchange of goods, services, and the accrual of money. Without money, we could not make much of a difference in the Earth. According to authors at Forbes, "*The Bible directly mentions money over 800 times and makes over 2,000 financial references.*"

I heard a Prophet say, "If you want to take a city, buy it." If the enemy can stop the flow of resources, he can hinder your worship and debilitate the advancement of

God's Kingdom. Although God does not need our money it is the avenue of exchange in the Earth realm. That is why Pharoah was willing to let the children of Israel go but they had to leave their resources behind (Exodus 10:24).

The man who lived in the caves was harassed day and night by evil spirits. The Bible says, "*For a long time*." One thing the enemy is aware of is those that walk in authority. In the book of Acts the Sons of Sceva, who were Jewish Chief Priests, were trying to exorcise demons like Paul the Apostle. Acts 19:15 says, "*Eventually, one of the evil spirits answered them, "Jesus I know, and I know about Paul, but who are you?"*

Jesus came taught us how to exercise our authority and execute dominion everywhere the souls of our feet tread. Below are some of the ways demons influence in harass people to hinder their forward progress:

- o Possessing people to cause them physical and spiritual harm (Matthew 12:22; Mark 5:1-20) and to make them do evil (Luke 22:3-4).

- o Blinding the minds of unbelievers so that they cannot see the light of the Gospel (2 Corinthians 4:4).

o Deceiving people by disguising themselves as "servants of righteousness" (2 Corinthians 11:14–15).

o Promoting false doctrine (1 Timothy 4:1) and performing signs to deceive humans (Revelation 16:14).

notes

_____
_____
_____
_____
_____
_____
_____
_____
_____
_____
_____
_____
_____
_____
_____

CHAPTER 12

SPIRITUAL MAPPING

SPIRITUAL MAPPING

Spiritual mapping is similar to mind mapping. Mind mapping is the process of using diagrams to organize information or ideas. Spiritual mapping is the process of identifying breaches in a person, organization, or region.

It helps you discover the root issues. In project management, I learned deficiencies in an organization are a people issue, a system issue, or a training issue. Once you identify what the problem is it makes it easier to mitigate.

Understanding the history of a company and the area in which a company is domiciled will also help you understand the enemies' influence in the region. Demons do not just like to control and manipulate people they like to dominate regions and control the entire city.

As we look at the history of cities we can understand how and why these spirits have dominion and authority. Before you start mapping your organization it would be helpful to map the city as well.

SPIRITUAL MAPPING DIAGRAM

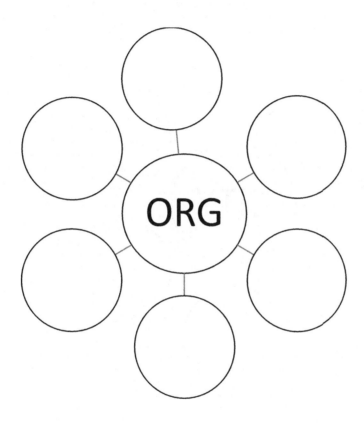

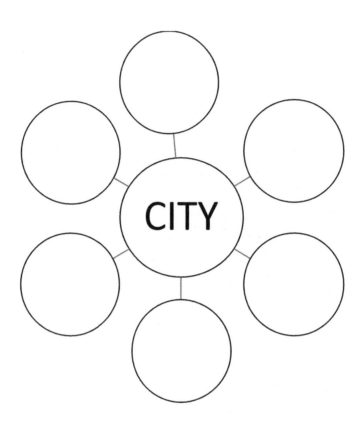

_____

_____

_____

_____

_____

_____

_____

_____

_____

_____

_____

_____

_____

CHAPTER 13

SURVIVING THE ASSAULT

1. Do not allow yourself to become a victim. Romans 8:37 says, "*No, in all these things we are more than conquerors through him who loved us.*"

2. Understand you are not alone, Psalms 34:7 says, "*The angel of the LORD encamps around those who fear him, and he delivers them.*

3. Pray for them. You cannot stay mad and fear someone you are praying for. Matthew 5:44 says, "*But I tell you, love your enemies and pray for those who persecute you.*"

4. Kill them with kindness. 1 Peter 4:8 says, "*Above all, love each other deeply because love covers over a multitude of sins.*"

5. Remember you are on the offense and not the defense. Ephesians 6:11 says, "*Put on the full armor of God so that you can take your stand against the devil's schemes.*"

6. Ask the Holy Spirit if there is anything in you that is permitting them to assault you. i.e., unforgiveness, rejection issues, fear, etc. 1 Peter 5:8 says, "*Be alert and*

of sober mind. Your enemy the devil prowls around like a roaring lion looking for someone to devour.

7. Strengthen your emotions and renew your mind. Do not allow yourself to become fainthearted or weary. Philippians 4:6-7 says, "*Do not be anxious about anything, but in every situation, by prayer and petition, with thanksgiving, present your request to God. And the peace of God, which transcends all understanding, will guard your hearts and your minds in Christ Jesus.*"

8. Rejoice, and again I say rejoice. James 1:2 says, "*Consider it pure joy, my brother and sister, whenever you face trials of many kinds.*"

9. Counteract the spirit of fear and intimidation with worship. 2 Timothy 1:7 says, "*For the Spirit God gave us does not make us timid, but gives us power, love, and self-discipline.*

_____
_____
_____
_____
_____
_____
_____
_____
_____
_____
_____
_____
_____

CHAPTER 14

HOW TO WIN THE BATTLE

Someone asked me, "How do I get rid of people that harass you in the workplace?" You do not get rid of them as much as you prevail over them. The word of God promises us no weapon forged by the enemy will prevail against us (Isaiah 54:17).

So how do you win the battle? Your primary offensive weapon is your Biblical declaration and confession. You must develop a battle strategy at the moment of identification, do not let intimidation cause you to delay or waste time.

The following are four keys to taking an active battle stance in the workplace:

1. Before going to work, spend time in prayer and declaration. Strengthen yourself in the Word. Psalm 119:105 says, *"Your word is a lamp to my feet and a light to my path."*

2. Ask the Holy Spirit, outside of the enemy, who is behind the assault. Many times, the actual perpetrator will use minions to do their bidding. Ephesians 6:12 says, *"For we wrestle not against flesh and blood, but against principalities, against*

powers, against the rulers of the darkness of this world, against spiritual wickedness in high places."

3. Be grateful. Complaining opens you up to the enemy and makes it easy for him to weaken you. 1 Thessalonians 5:18 says, *"In everything give thanks; for this is the will of God in Christ Jesus for you."*

4. Know that God is fighting for you. David cried out to God, *"Plead my cause, O LORD, with those who*

strive with me; fight against those who fight against me" (Psalm 35:1).

5. Take possession of your workplace. God told Moses in Exodus 3:5 (KJV), *"Put off thy shoes from off thy feet: for the place where thou standest is holy ground."* God said to me a long time ago, "Even if you stand amid devils, the ground where your feet touch is holy and restricts demonic activity."

_____
_____
_____
_____
_____
_____
_____
_____
_____
_____
_____
_____
_____

CHAPTER 15

MADE FOR WAR

My Pastor, Rob Covell, preached a message that I believe is crucial to where many of us are. He said, "There are things you can do to set you up for a breakthrough lifestyle. The Christian lifestyle is just that, a LIFESTYLE! It is choosing every single day to honor God and advance the Kingdom.

It is extremely easy to become stagnant, overwhelmed by life, and completely burned out, which is not God's plan for us. That is why I believe this is a crucial strategy to sustainable Christianity. I have been saved for over 30 years and it still feels like it was yesterday.

Every day, week, month, year, and decade have been a constant discipline in crucifying my flesh and choosing to do what is right. I have not always hit the mark, so I thank God for the opportunity to repent and receive God's forgiveness when I do fall below the standard of righteousness.

PRINCIPLE # 1 – Doing What is Right and being Faithful – 2 Chronicles 32:1

King Hezekiah did what was right in God's eyes. He was abundant in His giving to the temple, he lived a life of generosity, obedience, and diligence in the word.

PRINCIPLE # 2 – You Need Wise Counsel and a Battle Strategy – 2 Chronicles – 32:1-6.

Warfare always follows obedience; the enemy comes to push back and release fear. Therefore, it is important to seek counsel for a strategy to wage war. After seeking counsel, Hezekiah blocked the river, built walls, and multiplied their arsenal of weapons.

It is time to shore up the walls of your life. You cannot advance in Kingdom endeavors and think the enemy is going to passively sit back and let you move forward.

PRINCIPLE # 3 – Strengthen Yourself in the Lord – 2 Chronicles 32:3-6.

He reminded them to be strong and courageous and remember that the Lord will always fight their battles. It does not matter how fortified the enemy's regime is the Lord of Host is the Captain of the army. When surrounded by the Syrians Elisha told his servant, "Don't be afraid, those who are with us are more than those who are with them."

PRINCIPLE # 4 – The Enemy Will Always Use Fear to Stop You – 2 Chronicles 32:9-15.

Fear and intimidation are two of the enemy's choice weapons. He will tell you lies about God, yourself, your family, your spouse, your friends, and anyone else that he wants to break your strategic alliance with. You can never come in agreement with the lies of the enemy, and you cannot let what you see in the natural guide your faith.

1. Know that God is fighting for you. David cried out to God, *"Plead my cause, O LORD, with those who*

strive with me; fight against those who fight against me" (Psalm 35:1).

2. Take possession of your workplace. God told Moses in Exodus 3:5 (KJV), *"Put off thy shoes from off thy feet: for the place where thou standest is holy ground."* God said to me a long time ago, "Even if you stand amid devils, the ground where your feet touch is holy and restricts demonic activity."

notes

_____
_____
_____
_____
_____
_____
_____
_____
_____
_____
_____
_____

CHAPTER 16

BATTLE READY

The Holy Spirit has been impressing in the fibers of my soul that so many Christians are sitting on the sidelines watching the game or are on the injured reserve list. Christianity is more offensive than it is defensive. We are in the business of gaining ground and advancing on enemy territory. The gates of Hell cannot and will not prevail against you!

You have been made and equipped for War. The early Saints understood that church was an army, not a club. David, the psalmist wrote, "Praise be the LORD my Rock, who trains my hands for war, my fingers for battle,

(Psalms 144:1, NIV)" Christianity is not passive but aggressive. It is time to apprehend the promises of God spoken over your life.

One of the greatest revelations I have ever received is that I am seated in heavenly places in Christ Jesus. Because my life is hidden in Him (Colossians 3:3), when He died, I died, when He resurrected I did too when He ascended far above principalities and powers, I ascended with Him, When He sat down at the right hand of the Father, I took my seat!

I am not subject to the enemies, assaults, people's accusations, witchcraft, sorcery, voodoo, hexes, curses, failure, or defeat because Jesus released all authority and power into my hands to overcome! I am walking in my delegated authority regardless of the obstacles and the attacks.

I am not throwing prayers up to heaven I am seated in Christ praying from the throne room down and demonic forces have to obey me. I am confident in Him, clothed in righteousness, anointed from on high, secure in my eternal salvation, and walking in preeminent authority.

_____
_____
_____
_____
_____
_____
_____
_____
_____
_____
_____
_____
_____
_____

CHAPTER 17

PRAYING WITH AUTHORITY

Prayer is by far the most powerful force known to humankind. As partakers in Jesus' triumph over death and sin, we have received the authority to pray for others and to expel the darkness of wickedness and oppression. In prayer, we have been given an arsenal of weaponry with a divine license to destroy the power of the Enemy and thwart his assaults.

Prayer is a necessary discipline for every Spirit-filled believer. It has been the catalyst for every renewal since the beginning of time. And for every breakthrough in church history, a group of people committed to bombarding heaven's throne for revival will be found. In looking back through history for examples of revival, the Moravian prayer revival of 1727 ran uninterrupted 24 hours a day for 100 years, and in 1906 Azusa Street Revival, which touched the nation and the world, started as a prayer service on Bonnie Brae Street in Los Angeles, California. Prayer is not a random act of communication but a militaristic, strategic tool that aids man in bringing God's kingdom here on earth. His kingdom is a noble display of His power that deputizes every believer to walk in His authority. Prayer is a kingdom conference where we make known our requests to God, release angelic regimes, establish our authority on the earth, maintain our victory stance, continuously defeat the Enemy, pronounce our declarations of faith according to the Word, and then wait for divine instructions.

JESUS' MANDATE AND PRAYER PATTERN In Matthew 6:5-8, Jesus warns us not to imitate the behavior of the hypocrites who make their prayer life a public display for the approval of man, not God. As Spirit-filled believers, we are to retreat into a secret, private place so that we can only be seen by God when we pray.

In Matthew 6:9-15, Jesus teaches His disciples how to pray because He knows that His time of departure is imminent and that they must occupy enemy territory and advance the church when He leaves.

PRAYER PATTERN #1: "Our Father."

Scripture: Romans 8:15, "The Spirit you received does not make you slaves so that you live in fear again; rather, the Spirit you received brought about your adoption to sonship. And by him, we cry, 'Abba, Father.'"

The first item on the agenda is to settle any issues you have with your earthly father. Superimposing the natural characteristics of our earthly father onto God is all too easy. It does not matter whether your earthly father was bad or good, absent, or present, strict, or lenient, or distant or loving. God stands in a class by Himself, and for our prayer to be fruitful, we must see God as a loving Father. The name Abba indicates an affectionate, dependent relationship, so we should see God as One who protects and provides. Because we have a relationship with Him, we can enter His presence in thanksgiving and worship, not guilt, condemnation, or repentance for wrongdoing.

PRAYER PATTERN #2: "Hallowed be your name."

Scripture: I Kings 8:23, "There is no God like You in heaven above or on earth below—You who keep Your covenant of love with Your servants who continue wholeheartedly in Your way."

This declaration acts as an imperative or command, not an observation. God demands that we recognize His holiness. The scriptures insist that He is holy, separate, distinct, and set apart. He is God, and there is no other.

The Greek word for name is ónoma, which figuratively means "the manifestation or revelation of someone's character, distinguishing a person from all others." Praying in the name of Jesus then means "to pray as directed and authorized by Him, seeking revelation that flows from being in His presence." "Praying in Jesus' name," therefore, is not merely a religious formula said to end prayers but, in essence, is the manifestation of our status as deputies.

According to Hebrew tradition, a person's name embodies the complete essence and character of that person. The following are the redemptive names of God:

a. Jehovah Tsidkenu — God our righteousness (Jeremiah 23:5, 6)

b. Jehovah M'Kaddesh — The Lord who sanctifies (Leviticus 20:8)

c. Jehovah Shammah — The angel of the Lord is with you, you mighty man of valor. The literal meaning is "the Lord is there" (Judges 6:12, Ezekiel 48:35).

d. Jehovah Shalom — Gideon built an altar and called it "Jehovah is peace." By definition, the word means "harmony and reconciliation of relationships" (Judges 6:24).

e. Jehovah Rapha — The Lord who heals (Exodus 15:22–26)

f. Jehovah Jireh — Our Provider, freedom from the curse of the law (Genesis 22:14)

g. Jehovah Nissi — Freedom from fear; our pole, banner and the standard which declares our victory in battle (Exodus 17:15)

h. Jehovah Raah — The Lord is my Shepherd who feeds and leads us to pasture. He is a constant friend and companion (Psalm 23:1).

PRAYER PATTERN #3: "Your Kingdom come; your will be done on earth as it is in heaven."

Scripture: Luke 17:21, "Nor will people say, 'Here it is,' or 'There it is because the kingdom of God is in your midst."

The Greek word for kingdom is basileía, which means "the king's domain or where a king rules in sovereignty." The kingdom of God is His rule, realm, and authority, and He wants us to establish His kingdom in every area of our lives. We must establish the kingdom in ourselves, our families, our businesses, our ministries, and everything to which we are connected.

We establish His kingdom in our life by declaring His Word. We must understand that declaring His kingdom establishes righteousness, peace, and joy in the Holy Spirit in every sphere that we inhabit (Romans 4:17).

PRAYER PATTERN #4: "Give us today our daily bread."

Scripture: Luke 12:24, "Consider the ravens: they neither sow nor reap, they have neither storehouse nor barn, and yet God feeds them. Of how much more value are you than the birds!" (ESV).

Provision is probably the believer's biggest need. When we walk in faith, many times arise when we have to rely on and trust in God's faithfulness to meet our needs. An area where Christians fall short is feeling anxiety and fear over things we might not need right away, for example, praying for rent due in three months.

God promised that He would meet our needs, so in this part of praying, we seek our daily provision, and we are commanded to not worry about tomorrow.

PRAYER PATTERN #5: "And forgive us our debts as we also have forgiven our debtors."

Scripture: Mark 11:25, "And whenever you stand praying, if you have anything against anyone, forgive him that your Father in heaven may also forgive you your trespasses" (ESV).

Forgiveness is a choice that, if made, frees you from the grip of the Enemy. Lack of forgiveness is one of the ways that the Enemy holds many Christians hostage. The prayers of the righteous are powerful and effective, so examine your conscience before you pray and repent of any sin or harsh feelings you might have against others.

PRAYER PATTERN #6: "And lead us not into temptation but deliver us from the evil one."

Scripture: James 1:13, "When tempted, no one should say, "God is tempting me." For God cannot be tempted by evil, nor does he tempt anyone."

No one wants to experience trouble, but sometimes trouble is necessary for our personal growth. Jesus certainly did not want to die on the cross, and He asked God to remove that cup from Him, but Calvary was His destiny. God never leads us into trials that do not have eternal value. The answer to our prayer might come in actual exemption from a trial—"the way of escape" (1 Corinthians 10:13)—or "in the strength to bear it." Also, we ask for God's deliverance from the snares of the Evil One. The Greek word for deliver is rhuomai, which means "to rescue from danger or destruction." The word implies being snatched up by an updraft (upward current or wind) and lifted above the Enemy's grasp.

PRAYER PATTERN #7: "For Yours is the kingdom and the power and the glory forever. Amen."

Scripture: Exodus 15:11, "Who among the gods is like you, LORD? Who is like you-- majestic in holiness, awesome in glory, working wonders?"

This statement affirms the authority we have in prayer and acknowledges Jesus' eternal kingdom, power, and glory. We recognize His divine power, and, because of it, we can claim our inheritance in Him. According to Robin Dinnanauth in Let the Warfare Begin, glory is one of the richest words in the English language, and no single English word can contain it. In its fullness, glory means "honor, praise, splendor, radiance, power, exaltation, worthiness, and beauty" ...forever uniting us in an eternal relationship with our Father.

Things to Remember Before We Pray:

1. As we enter the place of prayer, the angelic forces are poised and positioned to go! They eagerly await to be dispatched as we release the Word of God.

Hebrews 1:14, "Are not all angels ministering spirits to serve those who will inherit salvation?"

Psalm 103:20, "Praise the LORD, you his angels, you mighty ones who do his bidding, who obey his word."

2. God already knows our needs before we ask. We are His children, and we do not have to beg or plead to have our needs met. As a loving Father, He willingly supplies everything that we will ever need.

Philippians 4:19, "And my God shall supply all your need according to His riches in glory by Christ Jesus" (NKJV).

3. We pray according to the faith we have in God. Prayer helps us establish God's will for our life. Through faith, we make the invisible visible and the unseen reality.

Hebrews 11:1, "Faith is the confidence that what we hope for will actually happen; it gives us assurance about things we cannot see" (NLT).

4. God's Word is established and provides the substance of our prayers.

Psalm 119:89, "Your word, LORD, is eternal; it stands firm in the heavens."

5. Our prayers are already answered. Once we have made our declarations and petitions known, we do not have to keep going back to God asking Him for the same thing.

Instead, we praise Him and give thanks to for what He has already done.

Isaiah 65:24, "I will answer them before they even call to me. While they are still talking about their needs, I will go ahead and answer their prayers!"

6. We pray for God's desires, not our own.

Psalm 37:4, "Then you will take delight in the LORD, and He will answer your prayers" (NET).

Proverbs 19:21, "Many are the plans in a person's heart, but it is the LORD's purpose that prevails."

7. Our strength and persistence in prayer come through the ministry of the Holy Spirit.

_____

_____

_____

_____

_____

_____

_____

_____

_____

_____

_____

_____

_____

CHAPTER 19

IT'S NOT PERSONAL

As we move into walking in complete victory, we must embrace the concept that none of this is personal. As a believer, we are in a spiritual battle and it rages on every front. In our homes, in our minds, in our relationships, in the marketplace, and even in the church. Instead of counterattacking the enemy, most people allow themselves to get offended.

Offense is one of the covert ways the enemy keeps you bound to your past; it makes you a victim. It is a trap that initiates a negative relationship cycle in your life. I sense you are in a season of great transition and progress. You have been hurt, offended, rejected, and ignored but you cannot handle this attack like you did the last one. Deal with it and settle the score swiftly, there is too much at stake, you have worked too hard, and you have come too far. Psalms 119:165 says, "Great peace have them that love God's law, commandments, and statues; absolutely nothing shall offend them or cause them to stumble (NIV)."

The objective of the enemy in this season is to get you to internalize this attack and take it personally. You must handle this one swiftly or you will give the enemy legal right to sow destructive seeds, roots of bitterness, rejection, doubt, and un-forgiveness into your life, which can take years to discover or get rid of. The purpose of an offense is to cause you to lose faith, tempt you to sin, knock you off course, make you lose sight of your goal, or cause you to take a route you would not take under normal circumstances.

Your counterattack is to PRESS, PRAISE, AND PRAY! Do not allow the enemy to encroach on your territory or rob you of your progress. God has promised you hazard pay! Isaiah 61:7 says, "Because you got a double dose of trouble and more than your share of contempt, your inheritance in the land will be doubled and your joy will go on forever."

_____

_____

_____

_____

_____

_____

_____

_____

_____

_____

_____

_____

CHAPTER 18

THE NAIL IN THE

COFFIN

Forgiveness is God's nail in the coffin. John 3:16 infers God loved us so much that Jesus was willing to die and be buried so that we could be forgiven and have access to an abundant and fruitful life. Ephesians 4:32 (NIV) says, "*Be kind and compassionate to one another, forgiving each other, just as in Christ God forgave you.*

Over the years I have watched the crippling effects of offense in the life of Christians. I believe it is not most people's intention to become offended; it certainly was not mine. I was caught in this vicious snare and demonic cycle for years because I did not understand the strategy of the enemy. An

Offense unchecked and unmanaged opens the door to unforgiveness.

We have often heard people say when someone is enmeshed in the deadly claws of offense, "You just need to forgive them." The Greek word for offense is *Skandolon*, which means a trap or a snare. That is the very reason why it is so deadly because no one would willingly walk into a trap, it is a trap because it is hidden.

What I have experienced is forgiveness is a learned discipline, and most people do not even know where to begin. I will highlight some key areas that I have gathered over time that have successfully taught me how to forgive and effectively and victoriously move on from the offense. When you genuinely forgive there is no emotional trace of Satan's lethal attack.

One thing you can bet on is that you will get offended, hurt, and betrayed. This was Jesus' instructions to his disciples in Luke 17:1-4 (KJV),

Then He said to the disciples, "It is impossible that no offenses should come, but woe to him through whom they do come! It would be better for him if a millstone were hung around his neck, and he were thrown into

the sea, than that he should offend one of these little ones. Take heed to yourselves. If your brother sins against you, rebuke him; and if he repents, forgive him. And if he sins against you seven times in a day, and seven times in a day returns to you, saying, 'I repent,' you shall forgive him.

I often give my testimony about running into my ex-husband's mistress. It was years after our divorce, but the fact remained that she still helped destroy my family. No one was more surprised than me that the hatred that I had felt over the years had waned entirely and my first response was to embrace her. It solidified to me that the word works, and forgiveness is possible.

Forgiveness means to stop feeling angry or resentful toward (someone) for an offense, flaw, or mistake. To Set-free, pardon, acquit, or exonerate. When we genuinely forgive the debt is stamped "paid in full." Many times, forgiveness is difficult because we feel that the perpetrator still owes us an apology, an explanation, or needs to acknowledge their wrongdoing.

History has proven that power lies in the hands of the one that forgives, the perpetrator is almost always too weak to recognize or acknowledge their behavior.

Below are the steps to forgiveness that helped me:

o Forgiveness is a decision. It is not an emotional transaction but a spiritual one. You may not emotionally feel a thing and can potentially still have hurt feelings.

o Forgiveness is a faith walk and your confession becomes immensely powerful. Meditate on what the scriptures say about forgiveness and walk in faith that the matter is already settled. 2 Corinthians 4:13 (KJV) says, *"We having the same spirit of faith, according as it is written, I believed, and therefore have I spoken; we also believe, and therefore speak."* In essence, faith speaks what it believes.

o Acknowledge the hurt. Forgiveness unchecked becomes bitterness and resentment which is anger and disappointment at being mistreated. Anger unchecked becomes rage and rage is uncontrollable.

Ephesians 4: 31 (KJV) reminds us to *"Let all bitterness, and wrath, and anger, and clamour, and evil speaking, be put away from you, with all malice."* And Hebrews 12:15 (KJV) *"See to it that no one fails to obtain the grace of God; that no "root of bitterness" springs up and causes trouble, and by it, many become defiled (tainted, stained, corrupt)."*

o Ask God for forgiveness. Repent of how you have let the offense affect your relationship with God and his people.

o Pray for them. A friend taught me years ago you can never hate someone you are praying for. 1 Peter 3:9 reminds us, o *Don't repay evil for evil. Don't retaliate with insults when people insult you. Instead, pay them back with a blessing. That is what God has called you to do, and he will bless you for it.*"

o You may need to move on. It is essential to understand reconciliation may not be an option. One of your Kingdom rights is to use wisdom. I remember saying to God after a long season of carrying an offense, "I am going to protect myself." And He said to me, "No, I will protect you, you use wisdom."

o Trust and forgiveness are not the same things. Trust is something that must be earned depending on the magnitude of the offense. Some relationships need to be over. An old adage says, "Let sleeping dogs lie." One of the questions I often ask myself about relationships is, "What emotional state was I in when I met them?"

If my emotional state was compromised or I was in the middle of a significant transition I probably was not in a good position to develop a new relationship. People with ill motives or demonic intentions usually, attach themselves to you in a moment of weakness.

_____

_____

_____

_____

_____

_____

_____

_____

_____

_____

_____

_____

_____

CHAPTER 19

PROMOTION COMES FROM THE LORD

Promotion is not something that is engineered by man. God looks for those who He has found faithful. One of by battle strategies while I was in the marketplace was, I was determined to enter the doors ecstatic, grateful and enthusiastic about what God was doing in my life and in the lives of the people that I had the opportunity to minister to.

I learned the word enthusiasm comes from the Greek word *entheos* which means, "An internal divine power; frenzy attributed to or characteristic of divine inspiration or to be God possessed." I was not going to allow anyone to take away from the me the glorious victory of the cross. I also had to keep in mind that this was a moment in time and not my ultimate destiny. God had big plans for me.

This is your comeback season. Man is not in charge as much as he thinks he is. I know some of you have been denied professional advancement and promotions, but your Heavenly Father has seen everything, and He is concerned about every single detail of your life. It is not about delay or denial but timing.

God has promised His people that no weapon formed against us will prosper (Isaiah 54:16). In Isaiah 54:15 (NIV) says, *"See, it is I who created the blacksmith who fans the coals into flame and forges a weapon fit for its work. And it is I who have created the destroyer to wreak havoc."* Psalms 75:6 (Berean Study Bible) says, *"For exaltation comes neither from east nor west, nor out of the desert, but it is God who judges; He brings down one and exalts another."*

Every demarcation in time gives us the opportunity for a fresh start. Lamentations 3:23 expresses God's mercies are new every morning and great is His faithfulness. Morning does not only mean that we are constrained by a 24-hour clock but signifies where there has been darkness light is about to break forth. The delineation from day to morning is generally referred to as the "break of day". John 1:3-5

(NKJV) says that " In Him was life, and the life was the light of men. And the light shines in the darkness, and the darkness did not comprehend it." I decree the enemy will no longer hinder or seize your new day and where there has been darkness the light is about to break, shatter, violate, destroy, and subdue it.

One of the greatest challenges as a believer is discerning when one season is over and a new one is beginning. Sunrise and sunset look the same if you do not know what time it is. Knowing the time is vital to what your response will be. The sons of Issachar were men who understood and could discern the times and the season to give the children of Israel direction and instruction (I Chronicles 7:1). It is our prophetic responsibility and kingdom right through the Holy Spirit to be as the sons of Issachar since discerning the times can determine the outcome and productivity of the next season.

Also, God will use these seasons to prune and correct. A harsher season of pruning will produce and greater season of fruitfulness. The correction will prohibit us from making duplicate mistakes, solidify our sonship and purge us from anything that can hinder us from going forward. Per scripture, God is a father that disciplines His children.

Paul understood the value of correction and wrote in Hebrews 12:11-12, "For it produces a harvest of righteousness and peace for those who have been trained by it; strengthen your feeble arms and weak knees make level paths for your feet, so that the lame may not be disabled, but rather healed."

In closing, I believe we are on the brink of a divine turn-around. Isaiah 54:2 pronounces, "Enlarge the place of your tent, stretch your tent curtains wide, do not hold back; lengthen your cords, strengthen your stakes." It is time for a spiritual comeback! If you have been lax, relegated to the background, fatigued, fearful, weary, and AWOL welcome back! The spirit of the Lord will once again infuse you with strength, courage, wisdom, and ability for the season ahead.

"*Destiny is not a matter of chance; it is a matter of choice. It is not a thing to be waited for; it is a thing to be achieved.*" – William Jennings Bry

"*Excellence is never an accident. It is always the result of high intention, sincere effort, and intelligent execution; it represents the wise choice of many alternatives – choice, not chance determines your destiny.*" – Aristotle

God has given every man free will and deeply engineered in the soul of man is the power of choice. In Genesis 2:16-17, God instructed Adam and Eve by saying,

"And the Lord God commanded the man, saying, "You may freely (unconditionally) eat [the fruit] from every tree of the garden; but [only] from the tree of the knowledge (recognition) of good and evil you shall not eat, otherwise on the day that you eat from it, you shall most certainly die [because of your disobedience]" (AMP).

God's instructions were a divine directive loaded with options. If it was not a choice, then no consequence needed to be given; "if you eat you die." Because God has given us the power of free will, we have more to do with the outcome of our own lives than we would like to admit. We choose to heal, we choose success, we choose forgiveness, we choose to harbor our past, and we choose to let it go. The list could be endless.

There are three voices that we can listen to the voice of the father, the voice of the enemy, or our voice. Wherever we are in life is the direct result of the voice we decided to listen to and follow. In John 10:27 Jesus said, "My sheep listen to my voice; I know them, and they follow me" (NIV). The majority of the convoluted state of affairs I found myself in were because I chose to ignore the voice of the Holy Spirit. I wanted my way instead of His.

Many believers today do not know the difference between a consequence and an attack of the enemy. In the Christian world, anything negative that happens must be the devil. Seldom do we re-evaluate our choices. The Apostle Paul wrote in Galatians 6:7, "Don't be misled--you cannot mock the justice of God. You will always harvest what you plant..." (NLT). During a difficult situation, the first question you should ask yourself is, "Did I sow this?

Pastor Andy Stanley wrote an excellent book called, The Principle of the Path. The premise being, if we leverage principles, they will work for us, if we do not leverage them, they will not work for us. As an example, He used the law of Archimedes or the law of buoyancy. If we leverage the law of buoyancy, we will float if we do not, we will drown. The Bible is packed with principles that allow us to live productive and abundant lives. It is not just a book to be read or skimmed over but, in fact, a guidepost full of wisdom and principles to govern our lives by.

God has given us wisdom which is the ability to live life effectively. Wisdom empowers us to make choices that are in line with His purpose for us. The Apostle Paul wrote in James 1:5, "If any of you lacks wisdom, you should ask God, who gives generously to all without finding fault, and it will be given to you. (NIV)" You do not have to continue to live a life of defeat, chaos, dysfunction, depression, fear, or shame you are, without a doubt, one choice away from victory!

_____

_____

_____

_____

_____

_____

_____

_____

_____

_____

_____

_____

ABOUT THE AUTHOR

Immersed in ministry and business for the past thirty years, Yvonne Camper, the Founder and CEO of Between the Porch and the Altar Ministries, is a change agent and a prayer strategist. She has a powerful gift of impartation and healing; her message is revelatory, transforming, and revolutionary.

Yvonne is not only a dynamic speaker, but she is also a prolific writer and author with three other books available to readers. In addition to writing books, she has also written for several online blogs, local newspapers and national magazines. As a natural-born leader, she has spent countless hours training leaders in both the private and public sector. She is currently completing her B.A. in Biblical Studies at the Abundant Living School of Ministry. Yvonne continues to pursue her professional endeavors, and in 2017 she launched her own publishing company.

In ministry, Yvonne has served in several capacities, including worship leader, director of the altar worker's ministry and a Bible college faculty member. As a trained worship leader, God taught her how to cultivate His presence on behalf of His people.

Her peers know Yvonne as an individual who lives a sacrificial life of giving and service. On February 16, 2006, she donated a kidney to a woman in her church as an act of selfless love and obedience. As a result, Between the Porch and the Altar Ministries was divinely birthed.

Yvonne is a wife, the mother of five and a senior regulatory consultant for some of the largest organizations in the nation. Additionally, she has served on several national and global boards as a change agent and global strategist. She has overcome the devastating effects of molestation, the death of a child, the premature death of her mother and divorce. To see her today is to be amazed at the wondrous work of the cross and the healing power of the blood.

OTHER BOOKS BY THE AUTHOR

Healing the Wounds Prophetic Leadership Transformed

Healing the Wounds Prophetic Leadership Transformed Workbook

Curando Las Heridas, Liderazgo Profetico Transformado

Geared for Greatness, 100 Things I Taught My Children

Get To The Root of It, A Guide to Emotional Healing

Assume The Position, 30-Days to Possessing Your Promise

Botched Election, How Did the Prophets Miss It?

E-COURSES

Managing Your Mantle

Purifying Your Bloodline

2020-2030 Prophetic Strategic Planning

Assume the Position Business and Prayer Academy

Made in the USA
Middletown, DE
11 May 2021